How To Get Five Ukrainians In A Dryer

Russell S. Woodbridge

Copyright © 2020 Lemberg Press

All rights reserved. No part of this publication may be reproduced, distributed, or transmitted in any form or by any means, including photocopying, recording, or other electronic or mechanical methods, without the prior written permission of the publisher, except in the case of brief quotations embodied in critical reviews and certain other noncommercial uses permitted by copyright law.

ISBN: 978-1-951730-07-9

DEDICATION

This book is dedicated with love to Evelyn, Sabrina, Lukas and Markus, our four children who went on the adventure with us and thrived.

CONTENTS

1	INTRODUCTION	1
2	HOW IS YOUR MOTHER?	5
3	THE BABUSHKI PATROL	14
4	PURSE, MURSE OR WORSE?	24
5	WE ARE FAMOUS!	37
6	EPILOGUE!	49

CHAPTER 1

INTRODUCTION

Yes, five Ukrainians actually got in a dryer, but there is a caveat. Let me explain. Part of marriage and relationships is the art of negotiation. Well, my German wife Ingrid successfully negotiated a dryer. Are you surprised? Dryers are not as common in Ukraine as you might think. You can go to an appliance store, and there might be forty washing machines but perhaps only one dryer, if you are fortunate. Dryers are available, but your options are limited in terms of choice, size, and price. Since we lived in an apartment on the 10th floor, we needed a non-vented dryer, the kind that supposedly mysteriously sucks all the water out of the clothes and into a removable water tray embedded into the dryer.

On June 28th, Constitution Day, a national holiday in Ukraine, Ingrid and I went out to look for a dryer. We entered a store, and oddly, no other shoppers were in the store. On a national holiday, we thought there might be more people out, but then again, I am confident that the word "sale" does not exist here. Maybe that explained the lack of people in the store.

I am also convinced that the words "in stock" do not exist in neither the Russian nor Ukrainian language. If you find a product, then you must decide then and there if you really want it because the next time you return, it most likely will not be there. When I bought our coffee machine, I examined the display model and then found the salesperson and pointed. Well, that display model was what I took home after they plugged it in to make sure it worked. If you have trouble making decisions on the fly here, you will end up with nothing.

Anyway, we headed over to the washing machine section, and there were about fifty washing machines and, I think, at least one dryer. There were five salespeople leaning on the washing machines, easily identifiable with their matching red shirts and black pants. They sort of looked like the washing machine mafia—Boris, Sergei, Anton, Ivan, and Vladimir.

This particular day I was not in the mood to play "find the dryer in the haystack" game, so I asked the mafia for help. I said the Russian word for dryer, and eventually, one young man understood me. He then called for back-up. In other words, someone who spoke English. He was friendly, and while waiting for back-up to arrive, he pointed out the three dryers they had. We hit the jackpot! Three! How would we ever choose? Though the back-up unit had arrived, this guy took over, using whatever broken English he possessed because he wanted to sell a dryer. This was encouraging.

At that point, Ingrid and I started to evaluate the dryers. The mafia had nothing better to do, so they hovered to watch the show. I mean, how often do you get to sell a dryer to an American and a German who don't speak Russian? I am sure they will be telling their grandchildren about this day. Grandpa, tell me a story. I remember a time, little Vova, when we actually sold a dryer without speaking English . . .

A crowd of staff started to gather. Two women appeared, one of whom was the boss. This was going to be good. I don't know why, but I had a feeling about this trip. The mafia was making fun of our salesman because he couldn't really speak English, but he was trying. The back-ups were ready to pounce to get the sale. At this point, I was feeling a bit sorry for the guy, so I started speaking German to Ingrid. I knew that wasn't nice, but it really threw the back-ups off the scent. They were stunned. They had no idea what had hit them. I think they yelled for a dictionary, but I'm not sure about that.

Anyway, our salesman showed us how this one dryer had a special program and operated in English. He may not have spoken English, but he was not stupid. We looked it over and noticed that there was a wire basket inside the dryer. I asked in Russian, "What is that?" He pointed to his shoes. Of course, it is for shoes! You put your wet shoes in the basket, attach it, and hit start. That could come in handy in the winter. Who was the bored engineer who decided he did not want to hear sneakers rattling around in the dryer? Maybe his wife requested that feature.

I checked the sturdiness of the wire contraption and tried to close the dryer door, but it would not close because the wire basket was in the way. Apparently, the wire basket was not attached properly. Our salesman was not going to lose a sale, so he started working on it, but he couldn't figure it out. At this point, each of the mafia took a turn, except the women who were wearing skirts. Each person stuck his head all the way into the dryer to check out the top, the bottom, and the inside to find some slots to attach the wire basket. The bouncer-looking mafia man was at a disadvantage because he struggled to get his shoulders through the opening. All five took turns getting into the dryer to look for a place to attach the wire basket or for a secret code etched into the drum. Needless to say, the view from behind was rather amusing.

During this time, I thought I had an idea of how the system worked, but it was way too much fun watching grown men trying to climb inside a dryer. At one point, I tried to make a suggestion, and I started pulling on a piece of plastic but was politely told to back off. I was not a professional. I thought, "Hey Boris, I went to an engineering school, and while it really does not help me when teaching church history, it might be useful now. I might have an idea."

After fifteen minutes of watching the mafia get into the dryer, we had to go. I returned in a few days and found the salesman. He was thrilled to see me. He brought me right over to that dryer and showed me the solution. Well, if the door closed properly with the wire basket attached, then, of course, I had to buy it. I have no idea how long it took them to figure it out, but hey, they did. At least they had something meaningful to do on Constitution Day, and they would never forget where they were on that day. Hey Boris, where did you spend the holiday? Inside a dryer. So, yes, we got five Ukrainians into a dryer, but not at the same time. If the dryer was larger, I think I could have gotten two or three Ukrainians into the dryer at the same time. But, in the end, the shopping experience was fun, and we bought a dryer that had been thoroughly inspected inside and out by the washing machine mafia, got our clothes 95% dry, and could properly dry my sneakers. What could be better?

Ukraine is a wonderful country with beautiful people. Our adventure began in Ukraine in 2009 when we moved to Ukraine due to work. I, along with my German wife, Ingrid, and our four brave children ages twelve, eleven, eight, and six, arrived in Kyiv, Ukraine, with a vocabulary in Russian of the words, da, nyet, and gde tualet (yes, no and where is the toilet)? Fortunately, we had coworkers who helped us get settled in and somewhat oriented. The next year, however, was filled with cultural moments and numerous head-shaking moments where we asked ourselves: Did that really just happen?

We did not know what to expect, and we could not have anticipated all of the unique, memorable situations we encountered. While there were certainly stressful encounters in our adventure, they paled in comparison to the friendships we made and still have with Ukrainians. As of this writing, we are still living in Ukraine and have adjusted to the way things are. Often, we try to make culture an issue of right or wrong, but usually, cultures in different countries are just that—different. Ukrainian culture has much to offer with its traditions, food, and amazing hospitality.

What you are about to read is some of our experiences in Ukraine. The country has developed since 1991, when Ukraine gained its independence. Despite this development, there is still progress to be made. When we arrived in 2009, there had been one revolution in 2004, and ten years later, there was another revolution. Many of these stories took place in 2009 and much has changed. Fortunately, the future is looking better for Ukraine despite the challenges. Enjoy the stories!

CHAPTER 2

HOW IS YOUR MOTHER?

Learning a foreign language is rather challenging, but we decided to learn Russian. Most Ukrainians speak both Ukrainian and Russian, and the Ukrainian language has made a strong comeback, particularly in the last fifteen years. One of the keys to mastering a foreign language is that you need to practice speaking it. In other words, you have to be willing to "put yourself out there," as my kids say. What this really means is that you have to be willing to be humiliated. I might have a Ph.D., but that did not help one bit. I sound like an idiot with my American accent. But I now possess a unique skill: I can speak Ukrainian with both an American and Russian accent. Learning a language introduces you to the culture and helps you understand the culture better. While difficult, speaking the language in your country opens doors, and in order to learn a language, you have to use it. Needless to say, people generally appreciate your effort to speak their language, but it can be rather painful, as you will see.

How Is Your Mother?

From 1991 to 1995, I worked in Frankfurt, Germany, for an investment bank. I wanted to be able to talk to people and simply live independently. This desire is commendable but not always advisable, depending on your language ability. I was trying to learn German, and as humorist Dave Barry noted, "Americans who travel abroad for the first time are often shocked to discover that, despite all the progress that has been made in the last 30 years, many foreign people still speak in foreign languages." Amazing!

HOW TO GET FIVE UKRAINIANS IN A DRYER

Anyway, my German teacher encouraged me to talk to anyone just to practice, so I did. I was supposed to be open to people. Of course, I would make a good German; I do what I am told. My German skills, at the time, were just about non-existent. One day, I jumped on the tram and sat down next to a sweet, old lady who was holding beautiful flowers. The tram started rolling, and I did too. I asked the lady, "How are you?" She replied, "Good. And you?" I responded with "Gut."

That was not too hard. Ready for the next phase, I inquired, "Where are you going?" Although it was a rather nosy question, I got by with it, and she played along and said, "To visit my Mother." I took a chance and followed up with another nosy question: "Well, where does she live? In Frankfurt?" The dear lady looked at me and said something I did not completely understand, but I did catch that her mother lived in Friedhof. I thought this conversation was going well, even though I did not know the section of town called Friedhof. Who cares? I have something to report back to my German teacher! I am being open! After all, she told me that I did not have to understand every word to carry on a conversation. I should not let a word here or there distract me from pressing on. In this case, her advice was utterly wrong— I needed to know that word.

I continued to display the profundity of my German: "Are the flowers for your mother?" She replied, "Ja." "She will really like those flowers." I did not get a response, so I figured I butchered the sentence. Let me try another angle: "How is your mother doing? I am sure she looks forward to your visit! How old is she?" By this point, the dear lady, a victim, looked at me as if I were crazy. She did not talk to me again. Within a minute or so, the tram slowed down, and the lady prepared to get off. I parted with, "I hope you have a nice day. Auf Wiedersehen!"

Although I seriously doubted that I would ever see her again, and if I did, she would never talk to me. Instead, she would probably call the police. I looked left out the tram window, and there was a sign with the word Friedhof on it. Eureka! I knew where her mother lived! Maybe we can have a cup of coffee and some Bundt cake together. Well, behind the sign were hundreds of tombstones with flowers on them. That is right. Friedhof is the German word for a cemetery. I didn't talk to anyone for a year. Forget the open to new conversations spiel. I did not report the incident to my German teacher, and on the bright side, I will never forget the German word for cemetery. All I can say is that if I died of embarrassment, I was already in the right place.

Punish that Printer!

Learning Russian was an experience in Kyiv. Early on, I was bold, forgetting about my experience in Frankfurt and the cemetery, and was now getting to the point where I was dangerous since I could not quite put everything together yet. One day I decided to take a chance and order a new printer from the internet since the prices were better than in the retail stores. I called one place, and they did not have the printer they advertised, but the next place did. I was making progress, but I was confusing the salesman. I meant to say, "I want to order a printer," but what I was actually saying was, "I want to punish a printer!" The only difference between the two verbs is an "n" or a "z" at the beginning. When the salesman was confused, I reverted to the old standby strategy-I repeated myself again but louder. This sentiment was sort of true since our old printer broke. In the end, the company was quite good to deal with, and they called me often to confirm the order and to make sure I knew when the printer would be delivered.

The next day the dentist's office called me to confirm my cleaning appointment but what I heard on the phone was the word for flight (airplane), which sort of sounds like dentist. We have a flight next week, so I was really confused for a minute. The lady was telling me that I had a flight tomorrow at 11:00? Huh? We got it sorted out, and I went to the dentist the next day. That was an experience.

You know how the dentist or hygienist explains things to you or talks to you when you have a suction tube in your mouth, plus water flooding your oral cavity, and an electric-power tool working? You can't really speak. You are in a vulnerable position. Well, when the dentist is explaining the procedure in Russian, it is even worse. I was trying to concentrate in order not to swallow and simultaneously trying to translate Russian. I decided not to swallow, and all I could do is grunt, "Nyet" or "Da." She was asking if it hurt while she cleaned. I think I understood about half of what she was saying. Anyway, I had to return in three weeks for part two. That much I understood.

But, in the store today, an elderly man asked me what drink I just picked up off the shelf. He wanted to know the name, so I told him. He asked me what it was, and I replied that it was mineral water and apple juice mixed together. "We like it," I said. He asked me how big the bottle was (2 liters) and how much it cost. I told him 7.05 griven (local currency), and he took a bottle too. I am not sure why he needed help, but it was great to help him and do it in Russian. There is hope.

Death by Grammar

Warning: Do not operate heavy machinery while reading the following paragraphs since they will undoubtedly act as a natural sleep sedative. They will work better than Ambien, unless, of course, you are a language geek.

The other day, I told our teacher in Russian that the Russian language is death by grammar. Since she speaks English well, she translated in her head and then laughed out loud. Really? You think so? If I had thought of it, I should have said slow death by grammar.

Now, what in the world would give me that idea? Perhaps just one small example will suffice. Take, for instance, numbers. General counting is comparable to English, and I have some mastery of the system because numbers are part of basic survival Russian—you need to know numbers to buy stuff like 200 grams of cheese or meat. The other day, I was able to negotiate in Russian a reduction of 300 griven off the price of two bikes. Oh, what a day! The sales guy didn't have to use a calculator to show me the prices.

The grammatical problem that slowly deprives you of your sanity appears when you have to refer to how many items you have of an object. For example, as one friend observed the other day, a lady was walking seven dogs in the park, but only one was on a leash. The other six were just trotting alongside since they had nothing better to do while roaming free in the park, a common occurrence here in Kyiv. I always wondered why they have the rabies vaccine available here, and now I know. Someone a long time ago decided to take revenge upon a foreign salesman or was bitten by a wild dog and contracted rabies. But I digress.

If you have one of something, then the noun gets a unique ending, and if you have either two, three, or four of something, then the noun gets another ending, and if you have five or more, then a third ending is in order. For example, you have odna sobaka (one dog), dve sobaki (two dogs), and pyat' sobak (five dogs). Even if you cannot read Russian, you can easily see that sobaka (dog) is slightly different in each instance. To make matters worse, since dog is a feminine noun in Russian, you also have to make sure you use the right form of the number one and two. And if this is not bad enough, this is only for a phrase like "I have two dogs." If you dare say, "She is walking with three dogs," then just forget about it. Just do not say that, or use a workaround, like "She is walking with dogs." Still hard, but the best thing is just not to have any dogs or pretend you did not see how many dogs were there.

The same grammar is true for years, as in how old you are. If you are forty-one years old, then sorok odin god (forty-one years) will do, but, heaven forbid, you are 42, then sorok dva goda (forty-two years). The name of the game is to race to 25, 35, 45, and then you get to use an entirely different word lyet but at least from 45 to 50, you can just use lyet and relax until you turn 51, and then you start all over with god. Of course, there is a crazy system of endings to help you along, but for every object in the universe, you have to use three endings depending upon whether there is 1, 2-4, or 5+ of them.

Today our teacher told us that we would move onto the next chapter in our textbook. I said in Russian, "Good grammar!" She replied, "Complex, serious grammar." And she was serious. We are about to embark upon a journey through the genitive case (possession), and the Russian speakers really like to use this case, and unfortunately, there are about six different ways to make plural noun endings, which, by the way, is how you make the endings for 5+ things. Isn't that special? Now, go to sleep.

I Am A Liar

If you are not a habitual liar, living in a foreign country will convert you. At a minimum, you will become the master of making things up. Let me explain. In language school, my teacher will ask me what I did on each day of the week, and she wanted to know what I did in the morning, afternoon, and evening. She was not being nosy; she just wanted me to practice speaking Russian. The first of many problems I have is that I cannot remember what I did yesterday, and certainly not six days ago. My brain was full of Russian verbs, nouns, and ridiculous grammar. I will spare you the details of the grammar for now, but rumor has it that Russian grammar makes grown men cry.

Anyway, there is no more room on my hard drive to store what I did last Friday in the afternoon. I am sure I woke up, but after that, it gets fuzzy. I suspect, though, that I was praising God another week of language school was in the books. But even if that was what I was doing, I did not know how to say it in Russian and, of course, I did not want my teacher to think there was a problem with her—there wasn't—it was the language, and she couldn't do anything about that. She did not invent it.

What to do with the assignment? Let me see. Last Monday morning, I ate breakfast and went to school. Monday afternoon, I went to the movies and played football. Monday evening, I fixed dinner, walked in the park, and listened to jazz music on the radio. As soon as I finished my statement, Ingrid said, "No, you didn't!" I whispered, "I made it up." My teacher caught on quickly, especially after I told her Saturday night I was at the disco and liked the vodka. I did, however, use lots of verbs and places of location. I have been all over the city, at least in my mind. Fortunately, my teacher gave me permission to make things up, so I was off the hook.

Another time that you might lie is when a Ukrainian asks you a question on the street in Russian, and you are not really sure what he said. I think he said, "Does this bus go to Nivki?" I used to always respond, "Da. Da," (Yes. Yes,), but I fear I may have sent a Ukrainian or two out town by accident on the bus with that response. That was not good. I have now added, "I don't know" to my repertoire. You just can't go too wrong with that answer.

Another time you may be tempted to lie is when you actually do understand Russian. The other day I made a purchase at an electronics store, and I was due 40 griven back. This was a good thing because then I would have some smaller bills for the kids when they take the bus to school. The woman at the register asked me if I had a ten griven bill. The idea was that she would be able to give me a 50 griven bill for the change. I understood her Russian perfectly well and thought, "Oh, no. Here we go again." What is it about small bills in this country? I can see that she has ten, twenty griven bills in the register. She is holding out on me, and I was not a walking bank for their store. Now, what should I do? Should I pretend I did not understand her? I refused to look into my wallet because I was quite confident that I did, in fact, possess the bill she was asking for, but there was no way I was coughing it up. I combed through my hair and thought, "Two twenties. Two twenties, cash. I want my two twenties!" I did not want to look in my wallet to know for sure, and so the standoff ensued. I stared at her, and she asked me again for the ten. I am not sure, but I looked down towards my wallet, fumble with it a bit, and then smiled at her and said, "Nyet!" I won that battle.

And then, there are those times in language school that you try to act as if nothing is wrong when, in fact, you are about to fall off your chair laughing. My friend had an infection in his right, middle toe. He came into our classroom to get the hot water to prepare a salt-bath for his toe. Apparently, he was going to soak his toe during Russian class while he was telling his teacher what he did the past week. Naturally, a conversation started with our teacher. She wanted to know what the problem was with his toe. Since he did not know the word for toe in Russian, we all received a quick primer on the human digits, one I will not forget.

The same word is used for both fingers and toes in Russian. Once that was settled, we then had to accurately identify the various digits. We wanted to find out if Ukrainians have ring fingers, index fingers, and thumbs. Of course, they do—they are humans, but do they identify them in the same way? Our dear teacher proceeded to show him the thumb, then the pointer finger, and finally the middle finger. Remember, context is everything. My friend was smiling, and for some reason, the teacher thought that he did not understand the new terminology. She had him repeat the Russian word for thumb, index finger, and middle finger while she held them up. At least she was holding up each finger looking at him. When he failed to pronounce the middle finger or toe correctly, she told him that the word Russian word for middle comes from the Russian word for Wednesday (sredniy palets). You see, Wednesday (Sreda) is the middle day of the week. I am telling the truth. I am not making this stuff up. When the lecture was done, and we were settling down, someone asked, "What is the matter?" I said, "Oh, nothing." Liar.

I am a Foreigner, Doh!

We think we are progressing in our acquisition of this fine, ancient language known as Russian. J.R.R. Tolkien once quipped, "I wish life was not so short. Languages take such a time, and so do all the things one wants to know about." Russian takes longer than most. Unfortunately, Ingrid is learning Russian in English, taught by a Ukrainian. Ingrid asked our teacher the other day if she thought that we would really be able to speak some Russian after a year, and our teacher replied in Russian, "Only God knows." I thought, "Did my wife just ask you a theological question? Did she express some doubt about God's omniscience? Of course, only God knows, but that was not the question. She did not ask you whether God knows the future; she asked you if it was possible to learn this language." Something was lost in translation between the German and the Ukrainian. I should have translated.

When learning a new language, there are the inevitable embarrassing mispronunciations that endear you to the natives. One day in class, Ingrid was trying to say the phrase, "This is your garden," and instead, she said, "This is your bottom," to the teacher. Ingrid also told me one day in class, "This is my toad," while pointing to her imaginary hat on her head. We all laughed. In the Russian language, there are sounds and words that if you were to say them in English, your mother would wash your mouth out with soap. Of course, the context makes all the difference, but it still takes some mental adjustment, especially if you were a choir director in the United States now living in Kyiv (just drop the "c" and "i" from the word "choir").

You have to practice what you learn, even though what you learn in the book is, at times, useless. Our Russian book, written for Chinese people wanting or forced to learn Russian, uses examples such as "Ban Lin reads Chinese very well." Of course he does! Even though I have not seen one Chinese person in Kyiv yet, I can say, "I still do not understand Chinese very well. Over there is the big, old, interesting Chinese wall." Another one of my favorite phrases in the book is, "I do not speak Russian because I am a foreigner." What Chinese person thinks they will pass as a native in Russia? In Kyiv, no one has ever asked if I was a foreigner. I wonder why?

HOW TO GET FIVE UKRAINIANS IN A DRYER

No one has ever accused me of being an uneducated Ukrainian who could not speak Russian. I wonder why? I have never had to announce that I am a foreigner, especially after I utter my first words. In fact, one day, a man ran up to the bus that I was getting on and said something really fast, but I heard the word "number," so I said in Russian, "Five" indicating the bus number. He jumped on and looked at me, said in English, "Where you from?" All it took was one word. I didn't even get to use my new phrase that day. I was depressed.

Seriously, I try to use what I learn. For example, even if I know where the metro is, I ask someone anyway. It is still amazing to me how many people act as they know, but they do not; they lie. The other day I visited a specialist who makes customized sole inserts. Since she did not speak English and I do not speak much Russian, this was going to be interesting. Nevertheless, we attempted to have a conversation. Fortunately, I had some new verbs at my disposal. She asked me where I was from and what I do in Kyiv. I told her I was an American and a teacher. She wanted to know where I was a teacher, which by the way, the Russian word for teacher only has 13 letters in it. I thank God I am not a woman because the Russian word for a female teacher has 16 letters. I can't count high enough to figure out how many syllables are in that word. It may be eight.

Anyway, I told the specialist that I teach at a seminary. She did not know what a seminary was, so I said in Russian, "Institute. Pastor. Church." I did not understand much of what she said next, except for the word Mormon. I sprang into action using what few verbs I had learned. "Why do you like the Mormons?" "Do you understand the Mormons?" "Do you read the Mormons?" "Do you know the Mormons." I used all my verbs up. Conversation over. I think my Russian teacher would be pleased, though. The specialist was very nice and patient, but I could not understand her. This is often the problem when learning a new language; you can say something, but you can't understand the response.

One day, I was buying some fresh bread. I walked in and mumbled zdravstvuyte (a formal greeting). In the beginning, you sort of have to mumble because the word is a bit tricky to pronounce. Since it was a hot day, and extremely hot inside the store, I said in Russian, "Today it is hot." Practice what you know. I told our building attendant, the people in the elevator, and the lazy dog parked out front on the steps that it was hot today. Apparently, I said these two Russian words too well this once. The next thing I knew, she was telling me about her grandchildren. To this day, I have no idea what she said, but I still buy bread there, and she has never asked me if I am a foreigner.

Why Russia Lost the War

Although I thought I had some ideas about why people get depressed learning Russian, I now know why this is the case. It is now clear to me why, on occasion, the Russian language will cause men to cry. Let me explain. We are starting to learn about verbs of motion. You know, those words that get you from one place to another. It is boring staying at home all the time. Unfortunately, these verbs are often used in everyday conversation, so you have to learn them well. You cannot be thinking about sipping a latte at Starbucks at Brier Creek in Raleigh, NC (who would ever do that?) while reviewing these verbs. Otherwise, you will get burned or choke by either the

HOW TO GET FIVE UKRAINIANS IN A DRYER

latte, your teacher, or both. The other day we reviewed a list of 40 verbs of motion and like the captain of the Titanic said, that was just the tip of the iceberg before proceeding to sink.

The main verbs of motion are to go by foot, to go by transport (car, bus, train, metro, bike), to fly, to run, to climb, to swim, sail, or float, and crawl. I am sure there are more, but you get the drift. In addition, there are the verbs to carry something on foot, to carry something by transport, and to carry something by hand. This not too bad until you realize that Russian verbs are like double-mint gum—they come in pairs to double the pleasure. You have to figure out whether you completed the action or are in the process of moving to choose the right verb of the pair. Did you get there, or are you still walking there? Furthermore, there are only 17 prefixes that you can attach to the verb of motions to change the meaning. At this point, your eyes start to get moist, but you fight back the tears.

At this point in the class, your mental computer starts calculating. If you have about 14 standard verbs of motion, times 2 to account for the type of action (the verb pairs), times 2 to account for whether you are going one-way or round-trip, times 17, you quit Russian before you start sobbing. I now know why Russians and Ukrainians have difficult lives—they have a difficult language.

Here is one, shall we say, pain in the—uh, I mean—challenge. The Russian language uses different verbs depending on whether you are on foot going someplace or going by car, bus, metro, etc., and uses different verbs depending on whether you are going one way or doing a round-trip. Every morning, we walk to school, so we have to use the verb that indicates walking one-way, but if that particular day we took the bus one-way (how you would take the bus in the morning round-trip to school I do not know) because it was raining, then we effortlessly sort through the billions of possibilities and select another verb. If I use the wrong verb, I just make up how I got to school so I can never be wrong.

I am curious. Why it is important to Ukrainians whether you arrived on foot or by bus, I do not know. Who cares how I arrived at your house as long I did and brought some delicious dessert with? The same is true when you transport something in a car or carry something in a bag while walking. Both actions require their own verb to indicate how you transported your junk. Again, who cares how I got the stuff to you as long as I did? Just make it happen. I told my new landlord that I would return in an hour, but I used the wrong verb, but hey, he did not know if I had a car or not. No problem.

I asked my language teacher about how to identify the correct verb for the delivery of furniture, something that is in my near future with a move on the horizon. I only have hundreds of verbs to choose from, so I should be able to do this (right now, I am laughing as I write this and thinking, "Yeah, right"). I assume they will use a vehicle, and then walk the stuff into the building, but the furniture is in the truck so ... I assume the truck will go back to the store at some point, but it really is just a one-way delivery ... What if the truck has to go back to the store for a 2nd trip? Who cares about the right verb? Then, I am in trouble because they forgot something. The guys drive the truck, but then they carry the furniture by hand into the building ... What if the deliverymen call me as they are driving to the building? What verb do I use then since they have not yet delivered the furniture but are in process, or on their way, hopefully on time?

HOW TO GET FIVE UKRAINIANS IN A DRYER

I am still not sure about these verbs of motion, but eventually, it will become clearer. Until then, I will just say, "I will be there" and avoid the verb issue entirely. I do, though, have a theory as to why the Russians lost a few major wars in the 20th century—verbs of motion. The soldiers could never figure out if they were to march out and come back or wait for a jeep or tank and what they were to carry and how to carry it.

CHAPTER 3

THE BABUSHKI PATROL

Beware of the babushka! As you may already know, the Russian word babushka is the Russian word for grandmother. While babushka simply means Grandma or Granny or Memaw or Nana (take your pick based on your location), it also can denote an elderly lady who dresses a particular way and has certain inalienable rights. Let me explain. The babushki (plural) serves an important role in Ukrainian culture—they patrol the streets for violators of babushka law. Actually, I should say they sit around and use their keen eyes to survey the area for ignorant offenders, like me.

Apparently, there are unwritten clothing rules on the street that the foreigner must become acquainted with lest he invokes the wrath of the babushka. I have not found a handbook for the appropriate dress code, but I doubt it exists. It wouldn't matter anyway—the way the rules can change at a moment's notice leaves the unsuspecting foreigner at a distinct disadvantage, like me.

Ukraine is definitely a culture of grandmothers (babushki). They are tough and tell you what they think. That is their job in society. One day, I was returning from the store on my way home, minding my own business when a babushka, coming from the other direction, said something to me. I made the mistake of stopping. I said, "Excuse me? What did you say?" I thought she needed directions. She did not. She proceeded to scold me for not wearing a hat. Unfortunately, I understood what she was saying, and I just smiled and thought, "Do you see my gloves and coat? Do I look like I am ten years old? Do you see any other people wearing hats?" Nope. I just happened to be in her sights, and she was just doing her job.

Apparently, it is the sacred rite of the babushka to determine how much clothing a person is permitted to wear as the weather becomes cooler. In the summer, however, they do not seem to enforce any rules, thus people do not wear enough clothing. I am going to file a complaint with the babushki council, but I digress. My language tutor said it is tradition for the babushka to ensure everyone is properly dressed. I can hear Tevye in Fiddler on the Roof now, "What keeps the balance in Anatevka? Tradition!" Anyway, the other day I picked up Markus from school, and we were waiting, unaware of the babushki patrol, sitting on the bench at the marshrutka stop. They tend to sit seven to eight on the bench depending on their thickness, but as I quickly found out, they are unified and honor the code, whatever it is that day.

There was a cool breeze that day, and the temperature was almost sixty degrees. Markus was hanging out in a t-shirt, holding his brown sports jacket. That was a mistake. We were minding our own business waiting for the #455 marshrutka when we were verbally assaulted. All of a sudden, I heard a pack of women yelling loudly, and, of course, I turned around to see what all the commotion was about. Bad move. I thought perhaps I could pick up a few new words for my vocabulary list, or maybe observe a babushka beat up somebody, or maybe see if the ninth babushka would fit on the bench. There is, after all, strength in numbers. They tend to work in groups, although they do just fine when they fly solo. The babushka outside our building will send you back in if your baby is not bundled up properly. She thinks that is part of her job. After all, It Takes a Babushka to Raise a Child.

Anyway, I quickly discovered that I was the problem, and we were going to have a showdown. I lost. The babushki patrol organized and ambushed me from the back. There was a cacophony of noise or, in other words, it was not pleasant to the ears. They were gesturing and shouting at me, probably in Ukrainian, everyone in their own way. Their meaning was clear—put the jacket on the boy, you idiot. What kind of father are you anyway? Don't you know it is cold today? Where are his gloves and hat? Do you want your boy to die from exposure? Fresh, cool, blowing wind is bad for you. You must not be from around here. Listen to us, or else!

It was a well-orchestrated attack. Everyone at the marshrutka stop was now watching. I tried not to laugh because that would have been rude. Who laughs at people trying to tell them how to dress their kid? I was going to have to face the music. Unfortunately, I could not turn up my iPod loud enough to drown them out. I plead guilty to avoid sentencing since, in their opinion, I clearly broke babushka law. They deemed the weather cool enough to warrant harassing any parent who had unmercifully exposed their child to the cool weather. I am surprised that they did not call child protective services, but then again, they pretty much already assume that role on the street and are probably more effective than the government. Well, I caved in this time to my fear of the babushka and told Markus to put on his jacket. He said, "Why, Dad?" I replied, "Markus, you see the babushka over there? Who do you think they are yelling at?" Markus had the right answer, "So?" As soon as he started putting his jacket on, the ruckus died down. I was set free. I swear they were high-fiving each other after I turned around, but then again, maybe they were just clapping.

The cold, crisp autumn weather has arrived, so the children are bundling up with what we think is appropriate, law-abiding, non-offensive clothing. I can handle another babushki attack since I have experience, but I would like to spare my children the trauma, if possible. Thus far, we have had no incidents as the children have passed inspection each morning upon exiting our building. I guess I learned my lesson.

HOW TO GET FIVE UKRAINIANS IN A DRYER

A friend with extensive expertise in Ukrainian culture pointed out to me that although coats and hats are required, gloves are not. This past week, I checked this phenomenon out. I used my keen powers of observation to watch people on the street and the babies in the strollers to see if they had gloves on. People here walk those babies for a long time, and it seems the colder it gets, the longer they push those babies in the strollers. It does not really make sense to me since Ukrainians have a fear of breezes, but then again, there are a lot of things that do not make sense here.

Take, for instance, apartment prices. We looked at a nice apartment with lots of space in a decent location. There were a few negatives, but nothing that we could not handle. The apartment had been empty for about sixteen months. In other words, the owner had made no money. You would think the owner might be interested in lowering the price just to make some money until the market improves, but this would be logical. Do you think he is interested in lowering the price? Nope. Do not worry. You will rent it out again in another two years, maybe. Anyway, I digress.

After a week of intense observation, I tentatively conclude that my friend was correct. There was something to the no gloves or mittens rule. I am waiting for the day that I get admonished for wearing gloves. This aberration in *babushki* law must be corrected. I will have to conduct more research, but I already have some theories about this lapse in judgment. Here, they are in no specific order, and, of course, since they are not scientifically proven, do not post these anywhere as facts. Here is my stab at it.

Why Ukrainians Do Not Wear Gloves

- It takes ten minutes to grab your change and metro tokens from the sales window with gloves on.
- You spent too much money on your ugly hat.
- You keep dropping kopeks while passing money forward on the marshrutka.
- You can't feel the warm air you blow into your hands.
- You can't answer the phone or text your friend about how cold it is.

Invisible Man

For extra entertainment, this story title can be sung to the tune of Billy Joel's 1983 An Innocent Man, the song they play whenever a Caroline Hurricane hockey player gets put in the penalty box, even if the opponent is bleeding profusely from being whacked with a Carolina high stick. Hey ref, it wasn't me! It was the stick! Anyway, I have discovered that I have a new power here in Kyiv, one that I did not fully appreciate while in the United States. Let me explain. One evening I headed out for another adventure. This time the mission was to secure the antibiotic, Augmentin, from a pharmacy. Our daughter, Sabrina, had a sore throat and her tonsils resembled the surface of the moon. I was determined to get the meds, which are available over the counter.

Well, I left around 8:50 PM, and the first pharmacy was closed already despite its claim to be open until 9:00 PM. I looked across the street, and through the trees, I spotted another pharmacy with a 22:00 (10 PM for non-military types) on the door.

I booked it across the street, of course, using the zebra stripes on the road, since I would never think of jay-walking in my new country. I entered the pharmacy, and a young lady was being helped at the counter, so I stood about 1 meter behind her (39 inches if you are an American), enough to give her some space, but not too far back to invite someone to jump in front of me. I am still trying to determine what the proper distance is here. It is a bit of trial and error, and I have made more errors than trials. If you stand too close, you get the evil eye, and if you stand too far back, then you will wait all day. I was not going to wait because I was on a mission for my girl. Super Dad was on a mission!

Well, there I minded my own business trying to figure out how to pronounce Augmentin in Russian. It was then that I realized that I must have flipped the switch that makes me invisible. An older lady walked in the pharmacy, marched right by me, and, with amazing timing, slid right in there as the young lady left. I should have thrown out the right chicken-wing to protect my space, but it was too late, and if you take out a babushka (grandma), then you are in major trouble. You will end up in the penalty box bloodied.

I looked at the pharmacist to get some help, but then I realized that I was invisible to her as well. She never even acknowledged me. All kinds of thoughts ran through my head, none of which I care to share in public, but I wanted to ask that pharmacist what kind of pharmacy she was running. Anyway, I scooted forward, hovering above the older lady who jumped the line of one person, c'est moi. There was no way this was going to happen again. I was going to have to get in her space in order to get my precious little girl her meds. No one else was going to come between the pharmacist and me!

Finally, it was my turn, and apparently, I flipped the switch and became visible. I contorted my face and lips and made-up the most bizarre, painful pronunciation I could think of. I imagined passing a kidney stone. "Aaaaaahhhhh Uuuuuuuuu Guuuuuuuh men teen!" Was God ever with me or what because the pharmacist nodded and went to the shelf and came back with the right medicine and with a bonus—it was the right dosage. Hallelujah! What a relief! I did not have to figure out how to communicate, "I need 625 mg tablets." I must say, however, that my non-verbal communication skills have sky-rocketed, and I am now a ringer for charades. It is unbelievable what you can accomplish with your index finger and a nod of the head. The pharmacist, despite not being able to see me at first, was very helpful and nice. But then again, it wasn't her fault—she couldn't help it if I had somehow flipped the switch to become invisible. Now, if I can just figure out how to flip the switch when having Nerf gun fights with the boys...

The Window

We attended a Ukrainian church one Sunday and understood about ten words, but it was a start. There were three sermons, eight special music performances, a few poems, and prayer times. The best moment during the service, or at least most amusing in my opinion, was when an innocent man decided to open the window next to him to get some air moving. It was a bit stuffy, and the building, although recently renovated, did not have air conditioning. No big deal. Well, this guy did not realize what he was getting into. You want to talk about a commotion. I thought the ladies sitting behind him were going to give him a major beat down for opening the window. The man relented under peer pressure, sort of. He closed the window but then leaned the window open a bit. "Way to go!" I thought. We need air in here to breathe. People spoke in loud whispers to him and shook their heads and finally moved away from both the man and the window.

I am happy to report that he did not close that window despite being an outcast. He sat there by himself and enjoyed that breeze. All the while, the man was preaching passionately about something from the book of Matthew and had a handkerchief to prove it. I have to say it was great entertainment from my perch in the balcony. Apparently, people at this church, and I suspect in Ukraine, believe that if you sit near a window and there is a draft, you can get sick. The man sitting near us closed our window and nearly cut off my oxygen supply. Being my first time there and all, I decided not to open the window and push the issue. I was, after all, inspired by that man down the front but also forewarned. Our apartment window in the dining area has a broken handle, and so the window has been cracked open since we arrived. I am starting to get worried.

Paying the Bills

In the era of computers, software, and the internet, one would think that paying bills might relatively easy, but certainly not in Ukraine. Every month, you have to pay your electric bill, water bill, heating, telephone, and whatever else pertains to your apartment by the 20th of the month. I really do not know what happens if you do not pay by the 20th, but I had an opportunity to find out. Let me explain. In our new apartment, we pay all the bills ourselves, so I had to be educated about the intricacies of paying bills in Kyiv. My landlord, Pavel, said he would show me the first two times, and then, he would cut me loose. I would have to put on the big boy pants and fly solo.

True to his word, he came last month on the 18th. He told me to always pay by the 20th and to go as soon as I received the bills in the mail to avoid long lines, a rite of passage here in Ukraine. Waiting in line is a fascinating experience. Fortunately, all the bills arrived this month. Anyway, Pavel shows me how to read the electric meter and how to fill out the bill. You have to be exact and write extremely clear, or the bank will force you to watch the Oprah Winfrey show as punishment. I made that last part up. They will not accept the bill, and then you are in a mess. I have no idea how you would ever get another copy. All they send you is this small piece of paper without an envelope.

Pavel suggested that I practice first and then record the figures on the real bill because you only get one shot. He had his bill-paying kit with him: calculator, sharp pencil, black ball-point pen, ruler, scissors, and white-out. It was impressive. There is a clear system and process of paying bills. I think the ruler was there in case the scissors malfunctioned. At the banks, they use the ruler to tear off the receipt from the bill. It is effective, and apparently, perforated edges have not been discovered yet. This was going to be an interesting process.

Pavel ran the numbers and double-checked everything. He was clearly a professional bill-payer and worthy of imitation. I, of course, took copious notes since the bill was in Ukrainian and made a photocopy. The electric bill was done, and that came to a whopping $8.00. I then asked where the water meters were, and Pavel said that there aren't any, so we pay a flat rate based on occupancy. What this really means is that I pay way too much for water, so we now use it liberally in the apartment. As one Ukrainian friend explained, "You are paying for your apartment, your neighbor's, the water outside the building." Wonderful. Well, at least I am doing my part to prop up the failing economy here. I asked Pavel why he did not have a water meter so that we could just pay for what we use. He replied, "I would have to install eight meters. I have to pay for that." Huh? What about that concept that each apartment might have a hot and cold water line to it off the main, and you have a meter on just those lines? I am still a bit perplexed.

Anyway, we then look at the other bills. I have a 75-cent bill for a radio. What is this? Pavel explained that in the kitchen, there is a special connector for public radio. So? I do not have a radio and cannot use it. I asked Pavel if we could turn it off or something, since I do not need it. Not possible. Next, I looked at the telephone bill and realized that there are three lines in the apartment. "Pavel," I said, "I do not need three lines. In fact, one is too much. Can we turn off two of the lines since I do not use them or need them?" Not possible. Pavel said something about the telephone lines were already there, and he would have to tear up the walls to get them out. Huh? By this point, I am thinking, "What is wrong with this country?" I tried again in my broken Russian. "Two telephone numbers. Close them. I do want them. I do not need them. I do not want to pay for them." Those Russian lessons are starting to come in handy.

Being a life-long customer has a new meaning now. Can you imagine the conversation with the telephone company? I would like to stop paying for two telephone lines that I never use. Sorry, sir, they were already installed seven years ago. I was not here seven years ago. How about if you send a guy, and we just cut the lines outside the apartment and take a picture? Would that be good enough? What are you doing anyway with my $10 for those two lines? I thanked Pavel for his help. He schooled me in the art of paying bills. I then headed off to the bank to pay the bills. The fun was just beginning.

I found a bank real close to us. I had heard that this place does not charge a fee for bill paying. This is good, but it also means that if I know this place does not charge, then a million Ukrainians do as well. In other words, it will be a crowded place. The first time I went, the line was out the door, and may I remind you, we have a real winter here. I am a consciousness bill-payer, but I took a pass on waiting outside. It was, after all, only the 19th, and all bills are due to one the 20th. Of course, there will be millions of people paying their bills on the 20th, but fortunately, there is more than one bank in Kyiv. Well, I returned the next day and walked right in, and there were about five people or so in one line and other people scattered around. This shouldn't take too long. Little did I realize that there was a system to the line.

Every culture handles line situations differently. In Germany, there are lines on the floor that you stand behind until it is your turn to approach the window, maybe even place markers on the floor, and if that is not enough, a guard with a Billy club who monitors the line and will throw you out if your big toe crosses the yellow line. In other words, there is order. In a place like China, the only place I saw something that resembled a line was at the airport going through security. You just walk up and work your way into the mass of people. I think some languages do not even have the word "line" in their vocabulary. In Ukraine, there are lines, and from what I can tell, some order.

At the bank, I waited behind a guy and stayed close because if their lines are anything like their driving, if you leave even a small gap, someone will cut you off. Things were progressing slowly, but there were two windows open, so there were sort of two lines. After a minute or two, I noted that my line wasn't really moving. There was an elderly lady with a cane to the right directing traffic. Apparently, the people milling about "knew" where their spot was in the line. The elderly lady, not an employee of the bank, was the self-appointed gatekeeper. It seemed to me that everyone was jockeying for position. There must have been at least six people who stepped up to the window when the babushka nodded her head or pointed her cane. At that moment, she was a powerful person, one who would determine my fate in the line. I wanted to say, "Mother, may I?" but I did not think she had ever played that game.

I was stalled out in line, and to make matters worse, the guy working the right window decided to take a break. The people in that line then merged left. Apparently, this is a proper protocol. After thirty minutes, I made it to the window with the babushka's blessing.

Everything seemed to be going well until the lady gave me the telephone bills back and a bunch of forms. I have no idea what she said. I asked her again, and I think I figured out there was something wrong with the telephone bills. Maybe Pavel and I ripped them the wrong way.

Well, the forms were in Ukrainian, and now the line behind me was about fifty people, and being a rookie in line customs, I was not sure if you get a do-over or mulligan. I feared I would have to go to the back of the line.

By this point, the babushka was gone, so the line was going to deteriorate. I could sense it. Now was the time to get out. At this point, the place was getting crowded. To make matters worse, the woman at the bank charged me 50 cents to pay my bills. Outrageous. As far as the telephone bills and the radio bill, I did not really care. I was a survivor. I spent my time in line for this month. I bonded with the people and advanced my knowledge of the culture. If I did not pay for a month, what was going to happen? One colleague did not pay, and they turned off his phone line. Oh, if I could be so fortunate! Maybe that is how to get those extra phone lines turned off!

Paying Bills Before Lunch

Paying bills seems to be an adventure for me. One month I went to the bank to pay and realized that there were 45 minutes until closing time for lunch. I looked at the line and then counted how many babushki were sitting on the sides and then counted how many people were outside smoking to estimate how many people were actually in the line. I then saw that two windows were open and figured about four minutes per customer and figured that I would make it. High math at its best without a calculator.

I like some risk and a challenge, so I stayed. I trusted the math and my instincts, plus I was confident that I wanted to see what was going to happen to the people who came after me. That is correct. There must have been about fifteen people after me. I came to several conclusions. First, they could not tell time. Second, they failed math in school. Third, they had more faith than I did. Fourth, they knew something I did not know, and the joke was on me. Maybe the workers decided to fast that day or something, and it was written in Ukrainian somewhere. Fifth, they thought I would let them cut in front of me. Yeah, right.

The bank manager made several announcements that they would be closing at 1 PM for lunch. It was so clear that even I could understand it. No one budged. Weird. The guy in front of me asked me to hold his place in line since he was heading out for a cigarette break. Of course, I played the part of an enabler and said, "Da." That is part of line etiquette here, and though if I had refused, he might have left and increased my odds of making it to the window, the sight of an agitated, fidgety Ukrainian in front of me for the next 30 minutes was too much to bear.

One time, I was at a bus stop, and there was a line forming. The young lady in front of me asked if I would hold her spot while she stepped away for a smoke. Well, another bus came, and I realized I was in the wrong line and had to leave. I looked for her. I really did. I waved at her and yelled, "Hey, girl!" But to no avail. Alas, never trust an American to hold your place in line.

Anyway, I digress. The bank manager came out again and told the people there was no chance they were going to make it. I liked her because she had reached the same conclusion as I had. She was doing the clients a favor, crushing any hopes they may have had of reaching the window in time. One gentleman said, "I know. Thank you. I will wait." It was getting a bit testy, nostrils starting to flare. The manager has done her job, but it was kind of strange how many warnings she gave.

What a tremendous feeling it was when I heard the lady announce that I was the last customer. Vindicated, I paid, and then the wailing began. There was a rush to the window and the women started desperately begging and making their case. I turned around to see if someone had died or something. Nope. No one was lying dead on the floor. Now I knew why the bank manager had been so diligent. She must experience this on a daily basis. I shook my head and returned home. A Ukrainian friend was at the apartment, so I told her the story, and she finished it for me doing her best impersonation of the ladies wailing. Apparently, she has seen this too. I understand too much.

Cash Society

Somewhere, I read a sign that said, "I am too blessed to be stressed." I have come to some conclusions about the person who started this trend: 1) he probably made some money from the signs and stickers; 2) he obviously never lived overseas; and 3) he propagated bad theology. Can you picture this? "Hey, Job! Do not worry about the death of your family, your poverty, and health. You are too blessed to be stressed!" Job replies, "Eureka! Now, why didn't I think of that? I could chisel it onto cooking stones and then sell them. When the cooking stone heats up, you can always look at your custom-made stone and be reminded that when God turns up the heat, you are too blessed to be stressed." Now that would have cured Job's weary soul. But I digress, though peeling off layers of bumper sticker theology is fun.

Life is stressful overseas. This is a cash society, so you need to plan ahead when making purchases. For example, if your delivery shows up and they hoist up to your floor and set it up, and you do not have cash, you have a bad problem as they say

HOW TO GET FIVE UKRAINIANS IN A DRYER

here. The problem becomes big and bad if you do not have the exact amount for the bill. As you may guess, and though it may be hard to believe, my planning failed one Monday morning. Let me explain.

In order to maximize space for the boys' room, we decided to search for bunk beds. We looked at numerous furniture stores in Kyiv for about two weeks and ended up going right back to the very first store. They were actually offering a discount, a rare thing here. The beds were sturdy, masculine –looking, and had two rolling drawers under the bed, providing a convenient place to throw, I mean store, all the toys when it is clean-up time. With some help from friends, we navigated the choppy waters of the Russian language without drowning and made the purchase. When the young sales lady asked me for my name, and I responded with "Russell Woodbridge," she understandably had a puzzled look on her face. I knew what was coming next; how do you spell your first name, or please repeat your name. I nipped this one in the bud and said, "Like Russell Crowe." Instant recognition! I think she even doubled the "l" at the end. It is very unusual in Europe to get the double "l" included in your name. I should have bought a lottery ticket that day.

We put down a deposit on the beds and were told to await delivery in about ten days. So far, so good. We returned home, and I realized that if they called me to tell me when the beds were going to be delivered, I would have no idea what they were saying. My daughters bailed me out. They decided that they too wanted bunk beds. Well, we returned to the store the next day and ordered another set in a lighter color with wavy headboards. The sales lady was a bit confused, but we made her sales quota for the year. This time, however, we gave her the phone number for our office. I am learning.

Before we left for Greece, we were told that the beds could be delivered, but, of course, we were going to be away. Through the field office, we arranged for a Monday delivery, right after we returned. The beds, mattresses, drawers, slats, delivery, and set-up were about $1,000, altogether not a bad deal. Upon returning from Greece, I called the office Monday morning to double-check everything, and no one picked up the phone. Hmmm. I soon learned that this particular Monday was a national holiday (Constitution Day) and the banks were closed. The good news was that if it was a national holiday, then surely our beds were not going to be delivered. Wrong. The bell rang about 11:00 AM, and here they were with our beds, ready to bring them up and assemble them, and I do not have $1,000 in griven in the apartment. Imagine that. This is a bad problem. My plan was to go to the bank Monday morning and exchange dollars. Now what? The delivery man does not speak English except he flexes a bit and says the word "Money." I try to explain to him that I will be back with money, I hope. I have no plan at this point, but I leave anyway, not wanting to explain to the kids why the beds have to be returned.

I go to the first three banks, and they are, of course, closed, but I think the ATMs should still work. I know I can use my ATM card and draw from my US account. I pray that I can get enough out. Up until now, I have only been able to get about $200 per transaction. I also fear that I will go over my limit, and I do not know how much I can get in one transaction. Well, the ATMs were turned off so they too could celebrate Constitution Day. Now I am starting to panic because when I return, those beds will be set-up and the men will need the money. I keep walking and go to the fourth bank, and the ATM is open. I have never used this ATM before, but I will forever use it from now on. This ATM bailed me out. Not only was it open, but it also allowed me to withdraw $1,000 and showed me the balance in my account when I started: $1,031. Just enough. Using both our debit cards and making multiple withdrawals, I had enough money. Thankfully, there was no one else around or waiting as I loaded up my wallet. Remember, though, this is only half the battle, although a significant half. I now have a wad of 200 griven bills, and I need exact change. I return home victorious to pay, and, of course, the bill is not a nice, round number. I now have a big and bad problem. Fortunately, it all worked out, and to this day, I have no idea what I would have done if the ATM was not so generous dispensing my money. I can now say, however, even though I am blessed, I was stressed. I can also say that I am also absolutely positive that Mr. Bumper Sticker never lived overseas; otherwise, those words "I am too blessed to be stressed" would have never crossed his mind.

CHAPTER 4

PURSE, MURSE OR WORSE?

When you move to a new country, you try to adapt and fit in as best you can. Sometimes it is impossible to hide. When I lived in Japan, it was obvious that I was not Japanese. When my friend and I get off the train in Kyoto, there was a group of middle-school students waiting for us to practice English. They were polite, but they had a really good idea of which passengers disembarking might speak English. In Ukraine, I tried to adapt my clothing somewhat so that I would not stand out immediately in a crowd. In other words, no baseball caps. Sometimes it worked. Strangers would ask me for directions and then be completely befuddled when they heard me speak Russian or Ukrainian. Other times it did not. My friend said that he could spot an American just by looking at their face. While I tried to change my clothing, I had limits. I refused to wear Capri-type jeans for men. I just couldn't do it. Those pants look nice on the female population but not on men. On the other hand, I had to make some compromises.

Purse, Murse or Worse?

Pickpocketing is a real problem here. If you put your wallet, phone, and keys in your pant pockets, you will eventually exit the metro train without them. When I first arrived in Kyiv, friends advised me to buy a murse—a man's purse. Are you kidding me? The truth is that even if you have a murse, you can still get pickpocketed, but the murse reduces the likelihood of such an event. I adamantly refuse to wear a fanny pack. There is absolutely no excuse to wear one. There ought to be a law against men wearing fanny packs.

I do not care if you are on vacation in Greece and have tons of money. Take your chances and get pickpocketed. At least all you lose is some money.

Anyway, what to do? I went to an outdoorsy, sporting kind of place to look for a bag. I did not want to risk accidentally buying a women's purse, which, to be consistent, would be called wurse. After all, I do not have any experience in this area. One friend told me that some guys carry what appear to be women's purses, and I have to tell you, there are some feminine looking bags being carried by men, and these men are married.

Shopping for a murse is interesting. How do women do it? Do you buy a bag with a handle or shoulder strap? What color? What size? How many compartments? Good zippers? How does it close? How much (who cares)? And, of course, how does it make you feel? I bought a blue, athletic, masculine, small, manly-looking murse from the sports store with both a handle and strap to cover all the fashion bases. Carrying a briefcase or leather business bag by the handle looks manly, but carrying a small bag by the handle, looks, well, different, but many men here prefer that method. I am careful, of course, to wear the strap across my chest as opposed to on the shoulder. It is a bit harder to steal, and carrying one on the shoulder is, well, strange, but again, some men prefer that style. I don't.

The murse does work well and probably discourages most thieves. With this murse, I thought preserved my masculinity and made the best of an awkward, but necessary purchase. I went downtown once without my blue murse and nearly lost my wallet. I had my wallet in my front pocket and was exiting the metro train. A man deliberately stepped in front of me even though he saw me coming all the way. "Danger, Will Robinson," echoed in my head. The next thing I knew, the man bumped me in the right shoulder, which, of course, caused my hands to move away from my pockets. Fortunately, I reacted quickly and thrust my hand back onto my wallet and his hand as he slid by and had my wallet. I turned, pushed him, and shouted at him in English. Do not ask me what I said. I then exited and went on my way.

I am sure he spotted my hand in my pocket, but many pickpockets look for foreigners. I am fairly easy to spot because I do not dress like Ukrainian men. I do not wear sandals with socks, mesh t-shirts, Capri pants, multi-faded jeans with designs on the back pockets, or white pointy shoes. I am working on blending in, but a man has to have limits. I can't get used to men wearing Capri pants. They must be the "in" thing, but I will not miss seeing them now that cooler weather prevails. The worse example is "faux" or poor man's Capris. One day I did a double-take at a pair of Capri pants. The guy had regular jeans on but had rolled them up neatly, making it appear they were the real thing. Please.

Anyway, my blue murse is small, and I needed a larger one, according to my wife. So, I have the blue murse, a backpack, a softcover briefcase, and now another murse? I guess I now have a sense of the difficulties women face when shopping for shoes—you need one for each occasion. We went looking for a black one, which is popular color here, in an attempt to fit in better.

You know you are in trouble when you try one on, and your wife says, "That one doesn't look too feminine." It was awkward saying, "Ingrid, how does this one look?" We found a black murse that could hold all my electronic stuff, most importantly, the tablet. We returned home, victoriously, and Ingrid asked, "Can I have your blue one?" Now I am wondering if I really needed a larger murse. When she later asked if she could borrow my new, slightly larger, black murse, I responded, "You said it didn't look feminine!" She retorted, "It doesn't, but I like it." I asked, "Do you want it?" And I thought I was buying a murse for myself.

Doctor & Leeches

Last week I made an appointment to see an ENT since I have been having problems with my right ear. My general physician recommended a clinic nearby. This clinic is about three years old, modern, and has new equipment. Now, of course, you can have great equipment, but if you do not know how to use it, then it is worthless. It is sort of like owning a Porsche and not being able to drive a manual car. Anyway, I arrived for my appointment and told the doctor about not being able to hear and the ringing sound in my ear. He tested my hearing and then checked my eardrum pressure with another machine. The doctor confirmed what I already knew; I have a bol'shaya problema (big problem) with my right ear.

This doctor knew how to use the equipment, but he recommended a treatment plan that was interesting, to say the least, and I am not quite sure about the diagnosis. He said that I should get an intravenous treatment for ten days. What kind of drug and for what purpose, I could not tell. I asked, but something was lost in translation. Step two would be some hearing therapy, and then the final component would be piyavki. I had to look that word up in my electronic dictionary. I discovered it is the Russian word for leeches. I checked the dictionary again, thinking that I had made a mistake and asked the doctor to spell piyavki for me. I was right the first time, but I had to be sure because this was getting medieval. Fortunately, the ENT could not conduct the treatment at the clinic but had to refer me to his colleague at the research center.

Sometimes the way they do referrals here is they walk you over to the other doctor's office. My doctor told me to return to 4:30, and he would introduce me to his colleague. Eventually, I met the new doctor, and he checked me out. I kept an eye out for leeches, but he decided to treat me with some medications and unclogged my ear by shooting some medicine into my ear through my nose. After completing the procedure, as he called it, he asked me if I could hear better. Of course, I can! If I say no, the leeches may appear at any moment. The procedure was weird, but it really did work. This doctor looked at me and said that we do not need to do the ten-day plan, and I heartily agreed. He gave me his mobile number and told me to return the next day for another hearing test. I think just the thought of leeches improved my hearing.

Internet & Moving

We moved apartments in the first year and, therefore, had about forty medium-sized boxes that, by the way, you could put about ten pounds worth of stuff in each one, otherwise they would tear apart. In other words, these were not UPS boxes. We sliced about twenty boxes and laid them flat outside our apartment door in the hallway so that we could bring them outside and deposit them in the garbage dumpster, conveniently located outside the building. For the small bags, and I mean *small*, there is a trash chute near the stairwell.

The boys think that it is pretty cool. There something about listening to a bag of trash fall thirteen stories and then crash and explode on the trash heap that fascinates boys. Glass jars in the bag produce the best sound effects, especially when the dumpster is empty. Anyway, the boxes do not fit in the trash chute, so we planned to take them outside. We went to a birthday party Saturday night, and when we returned, we noticed that the pathetic boxes were gone. Now it is possible that one of our friends took the pile down earlier in the day, but we are confident they were there when we left for the party. In the end, someone helped us out and saved me some time. Thanks. I now do not leave soda bottles nor used boxes unattended for more than a minute.

And then there was the issue of the internet connection in the new apartment. At our previous apartment, we had unlimited service meaning that we could download files without any size restrictions. When we ordered the service, we had to use a friend who was registered here already to get the cable modem and TV box since we were not registered yet. Apparently, official registration is a requirement for foreigners. When we were getting ready to leave our old apartment, I made the foolish assumption that I could just call and cancel my service. What was I thinking? You have to appear in person at their office, and since the contract is in my friend's name, he has to appear. Until then, they just keep charging you.

We went together, and we only waited in line for an hour or so, but fortunately could move inside the building after 20 minutes. All was well until we found that we had a special deal for six months. Of course, I was unaware of this special deal and was about two weeks short of six months. This complicated matters and is exactly what you do not what to do here. Things are already complicated enough in their own right.

To close out the account early, it was going to cost me about $40, but the consolation prize was that I could keep the cheap modem and cable box for which I had no use. Yippee!

We asked if I could just extend my contract until December 5th (6 months) and pay now for the last month and be done with it. No penalties, and most importantly, we did not want to come back. You would think that the computer on her desk would be capable of this feat, but what was I thinking? I paid up until December 5th, kept the modem and TV box, but have to drop off all the paperwork on the 5th. The kind woman helping us told us this was risky because she probably would not be there in a few weeks because she does not like her job and is looking for another. I can't imagine why. Hopefully, another person can help us in the 5th. But hey, all of this only took us one afternoon to accomplish.

I now know why people do not close out their accounts—they do not want to go through the hassle. Here, however, is what happens if you do not close out your account properly. You move into a new apartment, and the cable technicians come. In Ukraine, you, the consumer, honestly record the meter readings each month and multiply by some rate, and then you pay whatever amount you calculated. This might be a cost-efficient system in a country where corruption is not a significant problem, and the people are not so resourceful and clever.

Of course, this system is particularly convenient for the consumer when an increase in the rates is announced ahead of time, which actually happened last month; the price for gas tripled. Well, Ukrainians are extremely resourceful and clever people, and if you are calculating the gas usage, then maybe you used a lot of gas the previous month, calculated at the lower rate, and the following month, you used hardly any at all! In other words, you added to the actual meter numbers and paid ahead on your gas at the lower rate to save money. Let me be clear; I did not do this because, first of all, it is dishonest, and second, I did not think of it because, well, I am not Ukrainian.

Anyway, I know you may be thinking, "Does the gas company send someone to check the meter just in case sometime might be tempted to fudge the numbers a bit?" Yes, the company does, and at our old place, the electric company at least was rather faithful in sending someone to our place. The interesting thing was that she just showed up at random times, and if you were not home, she just kept trying. Persistence and dedication to the job must be have been developed in the USSR.

Usually, the electric meters in apartment buildings are in the hallway, but in our case, the landlord commandeered the hallway and incorporated the hallway into the apartment as a foyer. Thus, the electric meters for our entire floor were in our foyer. This addition to the apartment is a classic Ukrainian example of resourcefulness and is justified because no one else was using that part of the hallway, there was no one there to prevent the expansion, and it only caused a minor inconvenience to the electric company representative. Eventually, the representative came when we were home in the evening and checked all the meters. Interestingly, at our friend's place, if they were not home when the meter person showed up, she left a note to call her with the meter reading, but I digress.

Well, after nine months in our new place, the man from the gas company arrived at the door by appointment. Well, kind of. They call you the afternoon before, and if you are fortunate, and they give you a time range for arrival. For example, he will be there between 10:00 to 14:00 tomorrow, which means nothing, but it gives you hope someone will be there.

I invited the meter man into the apartment, and he just stood there. I repeated, "Come in." He told me that he was from the gas company. Once he figured out that we were not going to have to play charades to communicate, he relaxed a bit. He asked, "Where are you from? Are you from England?" Then he told me about his friends in the United States. You see, 99.99% of Ukrainians have a friend, family, distant relative, or a friend of a friend in either Canada or the United States. He asked me if I spoke any Ukrainian, and I told him that Russian would be much better since, of course, I have a wide-ranging vocabulary when it comes to all things gas related. He said that was fine, but he kept slipping back into Ukrainian. Who can blame him? He was happy that I knew how to say, "This is crazy" in Ukrainian, a phrase I used several times in the course of our conversation.

He informed me that he was here to check the meter. No problem. I led him to the kitchen and showed him the meter in the cabinet. He asked for a stepping stool to reach it, and everything seemed to be fine. He then took another meter out of his work bag and put it on the counter. I asked him, "Is there a problem with the meter?" He replied, "No." "Uh, then what is that old meter for then?" He told me he was going to change the meter. Za chem? What for, Yuri? We will call the meter man Yuri since that is his real name. He looked at me and said with a serious face, "You live in Ukraine, right? You are used to the Ukrainian mentality, right?" "Uh, yes, I am." I continued, "Yuri, you mean to tell me that there are some people who change the gas meter in order to steal gas?" "No da! Of course!" I pretended to be stunned at the revelation. I then asked Yuri if he thought I was stealing gas. He was confident that I was not.

I continued, "Yuri, if the meter works and I have paid, then why are you switching the meters?" He answered, "Because that is what we do. It helps against corruption." "But Yuri, I like my meter because it does work!" With my luck, I figured the old, new meter would probably have an issue. The "new" meter looked like he removed it from the previous customer's place.

It must be like musical chairs for meters. But hey, if it prevents stealing and corruption, then by all means. I was glad that finagling the meters provided job security for Yuri. Secretly I hoped the "new" meter maybe had been altered by the previous customer to save a little money. After all, did Yuri really check the "new" meter to see if it counted gas usage properly?

Yuri was curious as to how this all works in America. He heard that they had electronic scanners to read the meters. I told him that the company recorded the gas usage with scanners or even digitally and then sent me the bill and told me how much I had to pay. If I did not pay, then they turned off the gas. Yuri has heard about this from friends and really liked that idea. I told him that it is a pretty good method to prevent people from stealing or misreporting their meter readings. Yuri exchanged the meters and tightened everything up, and then I ducked for cover.

Why did I need to duck? Yuri was finishing up and thought it might be a good idea to make sure everything was done right. After all, you do not want gas leaks; and things can happen. He asked for some soap and proceeded to lather the sponge and then covered the top and bottom of the meter with the suds. Well, he put so much soap on the meter you would not be able to tell even if there was a small gas leak. He turned around and asked me if I thought it was alright. What was I to say to the meter man, the one who does this for a living? Use less soap, man, or get a gas detector?

I guess the look on my face proved to Yuri that I was not completely convinced that the soap trick would detect any gas leaks due to the amount of suds he applied to the meter. The next thing I knew, Yuri lit a match and held it under the meter. I backed up and ducked. He moved that match around, and when he finished, he looked at me and said, "Vse normal'no." It is fine. Apparently so, since he still had his eyebrows. I was thrilled to have such a meter man who was so confident in his work that he would put his eyebrows at risk.

He stepped down and was pleased with his handiwork. I thought we were all good, but then he said that he forgot the lead wire. What? He took out his thin wire and went back to the old, new meter and wrapped the wire around the bolts on the top of the meter and attached a green fastener. I asked him, "What are you doing?" He replied, "I am making sure no one can change the meter or take it." I inquired, "Yuri, who is going to steal my meter? Who is going to change it? Do you think I would do something like that?" He shrugged, "No, not you, but you never know with the Ukrainian mentality." I felt so much better knowing that no one was going to mess with my meter!

I told Yuri that I needed to write down the numbers from the old meter and the new meter to calculate the gas usage for next month. He said that he wrote them down on the document that I had to sign. I asked him why the new meter was not set to zero, but he was confused. Why? He told me that the numbers are right here on the paper, and you take the old meter number and add them to the new meter number for the total. It is basic math.

Thanks. I got it. Yuri left, and I am quite sure I made his day, and he is still talking about the crazy American who asked too many questions.

Vacuum Cleaner

When we moved apartments, we had to purchase a vacuum cleaner since the new apartment did not have one. We went to a few stores in search of a reasonably priced, durable, reliable, functional machine that would satisfy my German wife's Adrian Monkish need for cleanliness. In other words, this was a mission impossible. We looked at different vacuums and finally settled on a brand not made in Ukraine. Ingrid was happy, and so I was happy until ten days later, at which point the vacuum cleaner was called home to the great metal heap in the sky or, in this case, the great melting fire down below. It simply stopped working. Fortunately, the vacuum comes with a four-year guarantee—the company knew what they were doing, and I am quite sure I will need all four years at this rate. Prior to other electronic purchases, several Ukrainians told us to keep all original packaging for two weeks, and we obeyed. They have more experience with electronics than we do.

Now, I know what you are thinking. Just take it back to the store and get a new one or your money back. Within the first two weeks, this might be possible but unlikely. The store sends you to the service center in most cases. Of course, the service center is probably located in a completely different part of the city. Also, since you probably bought the only model, the store providing or even having a replacement is also unlikely. I looked up the service center in Kyiv so I could take the machine there and cash in that precious four-year guarantee. With a friend, I successfully dropped the machine off after waiting in a long line, a rite of passage here in Ukraine. The place was full of repaired items, and I took note of the large quantity of items by a certain manufacturer and breathed a sigh of relief that I have not bought that brand. All I had to do now was wait for a phone call within two weeks. Yeah, right.

After two weeks went by, I tried to call and find out where my vacuum cleaner was. I was not successful though I had perfected the phrase in Russian, "I need my vacuum cleaner today!" In the meantime, we borrowed a friend's vacuum, and it broke while we used it. It is contagious. I was starting to get worried that our vacuum was going to end up in service center limbo, so we had our language teacher call. We found out that the service center was waiting for a part to come in. How long will that take? No one seems to know. It will arrive when it arrives.

The lady at the service center said that we could live without a vacuum for a month or so. She obviously has never met my German wife, who has a hatred of dirt and dust.

Another week passed, and we decided we wanted our money back. To do so, I have to go to the service center, fill out a form, wait for a decision, go back to the service to get a piece of paper, and then return to the original store. Did you get all that? I went to the service center and asked for the form. The man gave me the form that was all in Ukrainian, not that it would have helped that much if it had been in Russian. He helped me fill it out, and when we came to the last line, he said something in Russian, and I had no idea what he said. I looked at him and just shook my head and gave him the pen. To this day, I have no idea what I said on the form, but he seemed satisfied.

I never heard back about the form, so we called again. Amazingly, though we had no decision on the money refund, the mysterious part arrived, and the vacuum would be ready in a day or so. Whatever. Three days later, I received a phone call, and allegedly our machine had been revived, and I could pick it up the next day. I drive out there with great hope and picked-up the vacuum after, of course, having the man plug it in to ensure that it worked. Success. I wanted to spare myself a trip to the emergency room, which would have been necessary if Ingrid had plugged in the vacuum cleaner at home, and it did not work. Fortunately, the cleanliness standards of our apartment have been restored, and Mrs. Monk can sleep at night.

The Haircut

Getting a haircut in another country can be a real adventure. Let me explain. I had my hair cut real short right before we left for Kyiv so that I would not have to deal with the quaff for at least eight weeks. Getting a haircut with limited language skills is rather interesting.

Fortunately, in my case, my hair always grows back, so I cannot go too wrong. Mistakes will be covered up eventually.

The first time I got my hair cut, the lady asked me something, and I said in Russian, "A little bit." The problem was that I did not know if I just told her to take a little off or to cut my hair to a very short length. Why didn't I just say I do not understand? I waited to see if I was going to end up looking like a Georgia peach. When she did not pick-up the clippers right away, I figured I was going to be fine. Well, she took her time and then blow-dried it, giving me an Elvis-look in the front—wavy, straight back over the top. It was a bit odd, and I started singing, "One for the money, two for the show." Not really, but I thought it. Now, if only she had dyed my hair black. I paid her about $6 and left. When I arrived home, the kids looked at me and said, "Dad, why is your hair so poofy?" Because I can't speak Russian.

HOW TO GET FIVE UKRAINIANS IN A DRYER

The other day I ventured into a new salon near our new apartment. There are salons everywhere in Kyiv. Maybe there is a law that requires Ukrainians to only have to walk five minutes to get a haircut. Makes sense in the winter, I guess. The good news is that I now can actually ask for a hair cut in Russian and figure out if they have time right away and, of course, ask how much it costs and actually knows how much it costs instead of giving a polite nod as if I understood the amount. This is much better than my previous method—taking my pointer and middle fingers, opening and closing them by my head, thereby creating imaginary scissors cutting my hair. I think my girls used to do this with their dolls when they were two years old.

Anyway, we get started, and Anna starts speaking to me in Russian and asks, "How do you want your hair?" I do not have the skills to describe in exquisite detail how I would like for my locks to look upon completion of the task, so not too short has to do and, of course, invoking the imaginary scissors cutting around my hears and off the back of the collar. Maybe next time I can relay this information in Russian, but I doubt it.

Maybe when I get a good haircut, I will take a picture right away and bring it with me. It amazes me that even though the hair professional sees my hair upon entering the salon, she manages to create something different when I leave. They go blind for a minute when you enter and then sit in the chair, or there is something wrong with their memory. If my part was on the left when I entered, then most likely, it should be there after the haircut, right? But in the end, they ask, "Which side do you want the part?" I thought you were cutting my hair for the left-side part but maybe not. I am not sure if they think the part should be somewhere else and they are politely calling me a fashion idiot, or if they really want me to feel involved in the process even though all I did was just sit there staring at myself in the huge mirror for an hour. By the way, this is why I prefer the twenty-minute haircut.

Anyway, everything seems to take longer here, and Anna is no exception—she takes her sweet time, and I do not think she missed a single hair. I must have been in the chair for at least an hour, plus she thought my hair needed to be washed twice. She finally said in English, "You have many, many hairs." Thank you for noticing. I think she spent most of the time thinning my hair, which at my age is a good problem to have. I lost a pound and can now jump long puddles in a single bound.

Anna also told me that my hair color does not look good. I replied in Russian, "Normal. Natural." She shook her head, "It is not normal. You have different colors." She meant I had quite a rainbow: gray, silver, white, brown, and a touch of red. She then continued, "You should dye your hair. It is very fashionable today for men your age to dye their hair. It only takes ten minutes for men." Really? You don't say? Well, I played along and asked in Russian, "How much?" She brought the catalog to me and showed me the camouflage option.

I wondered if that was different shades of green. Hey, it could be fashionable in Kyiv for men my age. Anna asked in Russian if I understood the options. I said in Russian, "I understand the word camouflage." She asked, "How do you say this word in English." Oh, it is really difficult. I am not sure if you can handle it—camouflage. I exercised some diplomatic tactics since the cut was not yet finished and said—I will think about it. She said, "You think so?" Uh, no. I will think about it means maybe next time, or I just thought about it for a nanosecond and decided not to go with the camouflage option. She took the news pretty well.

She finished up and before unleashing the blow dryer and gel, asked if I wanted my hair combed forward on the top and sides as opposed to straight down and back. At least she knew where the part was, and I now know how to say in Russian, "Same style but shorter."

The Dentist

I am not sure how I attract more than my share of random events in life, but I suspect it has something to do with the fact that I live in Kyiv. I survived the dentist once but knew I had to go again to finish the cleaning. The dentist decided that I had endured enough during the first phase of cleaning, thus the second appointment. On Saturday morning, I went with Sabrina to the orthodontist (same office as the dentist), and her orthodontist told me that the dentist no longer cleans teeth on Saturday, the day of my next appointment, but only on Sundays. What? The must be a law against dental work on Sundays. Who goes to the dentist on Sunday? Or any day for that matter? I was perplexed, but I think that the dental hygienist works an extra day at this practice to make some extra money.

I still needed part two of the cleaning (polish and fluoride treatment), but I feared if I got my teeth cleaned on a Sunday, God would cause my teeth to rot. Who gets their teeth cleaned on Sunday? Apparently, some Ukrainians. This was a tough decision, but I did not want to start over with another practice at this stage. I asked, "Can I have an appointment early in the morning?" No problem. How about tomorrow at 9:15? That will work fine since the church does not start until 12:00 PM.

Please do not ask me why our church starts at 12:00 PM. I have no idea, and I will not digress. Anyway, I arrived at 9:15 AM and approached the office and saw four of the hygienists standing outside. I said in Russian, "Good morning." Irina told me that there was a slight problem. I quickly interjected in Russian, "Who has the key?" She answered, "The receptionist has the key, and she is delayed." I thought, "What you really mean is that she overslept or did not know it was her shift this morning, right?" Two more workers appeared, and then I was standing on the street with six young women waiting for the key. Can you say awkward in Russian? Never mind, I can't either.

Fortunately, within a few minutes, the lead orthodontist arrived with Andre, the mystery man. I still do not know what he does at the practice.

She came right up to me and said there was a problem. You think? Apparently, this was the first time this had ever happened. I asked why there is not more than one key, and something got lost in translation, but either there is a law against having more than one key or it is a unique door, and they cannot replicate the key. I hope the latter is the reason. I was simply confused. The orthodontist invited all of us to a nearby restaurant for coffee. I asked, "Is Andre coming?" He was coming, so, having nothing better to do, I went along. We sat down at a table, and Andre asked me if I wanted something to eat, like a sandwich. He was just trying to be friendly, but I told him that I was getting my teeth cleaned, and it might not be a good idea (especially with Katja, the dental hygienist sitting right there). Oh, and I forgot my toothbrush at home. Andre said, "No problem. We can clean your teeth afterward." The idea of someone else brushing my teeth was more than I could handle, and I lost my appetite. I'll pass just the same. I wonder if they are model citizens of the dental community and carry toothbrushes with them everywhere they go? None of them ordered food, so either they were not hungry, or they forgot their toothbrushes as well. Anyway, I settled for a cappuccino and some conversation.

I drank my cappuccino, and we talked about traveling to different countries. This group really liked Paris and wanted to know if I spoke French. Well, I studied it for four years in high school, which means I can't. Andre told me in French that the language is not easy. "Well, actually, it is much easier to learn than Russian," I countered. We then decided that it depends on which language you start from as your base. Who knows, but I wanted to get my teeth cleaned.

The receptionist arrived and opened the office. As I waited, the head orthodontist told me that the cleaning was free today. She was extremely nice and apologetic. I then asked her about this Air-Flow cleaning treatment. I still was not sure what it was exactly. She assured me that it is pleasant and wonderful for the teeth. It gives the teeth a nice sensation. Well, this could turn out alright. Full of anticipation of my teeth being bathed in Air-Flow, Katja ushered me into the room and started explaining in Russian what process I was going to voluntarily be subjected to over the next 30 minutes. All I said was, "Air-Flow? Da?"

Well, I am not exactly sure how to describe Air-Flow. It is kind of like using a small sand-blaster tool on your teeth with a lemon scent. I was kind of disappointed I did not get to choose different flavors, but I had more important things to worry about. When they handed me the goggles to wear and covered me up to my waist with plastic, I started to get a bit concerned. Polishing teeth should not result in splatter two to three feet away. I had a bad feeling about this, and it was a good thing I was covered up. When Katja started, it was all hands on deck. I just tried to survive, but stuff was ricocheting when the stuff (baking soda kind of stuff) came out of the sandblaster tool at 200 mph and hit my teeth. The short of the story is that Air-Flow is evil, and the sandblaster tool cuts your gums. I never knew I had such long teeth, but I do now, thanks to Air-Flow. Amazing what a little gum removal can do. Katja told me that my gums would be fine in a few hours but that now I have very clean smooth teeth. Yea! All I could think of was now I have to go to church, and I can't even smile. At least it was free.

CHAPTER 5

WE ARE FAMOUS!

Living in another country is interesting, challenging, and certainly changes you. Your vision of the world is larger, and your understanding of culture increases. You learn to be flexible and to adapt to a new life. You also enjoy the experiences and friends. The best part of Ukraine is our friends. They have been so warm, hospitable, and gracious. Wherever you go, the people that you get to know to impact your view and experience of the culture and country. While the cultural shock and trying to figure out how things work is frustrating, it is worth the hassle, especially if you survive that first year. Most of our crazy situations happened within that first year, and then we adjusted, became better in the language, and accepted our new normal. I suspect we didn't notice as much after getting used to the way things are. Some things are better, some things worse, and other things are just different.

We are Famous!

We are officially famous in Ukraine now. Well, sort of. The picture on the next page was taken by our friend, Joe Ragan, while driving through Kremenchuk on his way to Kyiv. The caption on the billboard says in Ukrainian something like "Solid Family – Strong Ukraine", which made us laugh even harder. Apparently, I did not look like a Cossack or Ukrainian, so they changed my facial hair. Take a close look at my mouth. We are waiting to see this advertisement in Kyiv and are grateful that we are not advertising for vodka or something else. And no, we had no idea our photo was ripped off for the billboard. Someone said that we could take them to court. Now that is really funny, if you know how the courts operate in Ukraine.

Going Up?

I discovered another word that does not exist in the Russian language, at least not in Kyiv, and that is, safety inspector. I do not think the city has that department. They should, though, since it would create jobs. Let me explain. In Kyiv, elevators can be both an adventure and dangerous. In the US, I always wondered why there was a picture of the commissioner of NCDOL, the person ultimately responsible for elevator inspections, in each elevator in the state of North Carolina. Is that really necessary? Am I supposed to recognize her at Walmart and be ready to report any problems with the elevator in my office building at the seminary? That is right up there with having your picture hanging on the wall at the post office.

The thing is, though, I wish they had a picture of the commissioner responsible for elevator inspections in Kyiv posted in each and every elevator. I would memorize what he or she looked like and track that person down and report problems. And at least there would be a little piece of paper that the inspector signed every six months, thereby giving me some sense of confidence that the elevator will work properly because at this point, after four months in Kyiv, I do not have that sense of confidence that every citizen is entitled to, and for good reason, I might add.

The elevator technology in most residential buildings is at least forty years old. I am not saying the elevators are never inspected, but if they are, then someone needs to be fired. It is never a good feeling when you step into the elevator, and it rocks slightly. In our friend's building, we have to spread out in the elevator or lift to distribute the weight evenly because, in the past, the elevator has become wedged in the shaft due to the tilt. I thought he was joking, but he was not, and since I could see down through the door into the shaft due to the gaping crack, we spread out. Next time, I will bring a portable scale. I now have some new Boy Scout mottos:

Be courteous and smart—always let a big person start. Do not worry and do not be rushed—the elevator will return, and you will not be crushed.

When getting on the elevator, you have to watch out for the closing doors. The doors in our elevators still close if you are in the way, and they close hard. There isn't a safety feature that tells the door to back-off if you just happen to be getting on. I was, unfortunately, stepping onto the uninspected lift when the doors tried to take me out. Although I have never been hit by an NFL linebacker, I think I have a good idea now what that feels like, and I did not have any pads on. Those doors tried to tackle me, but I did not go down! I was crushed, staggering, and singing, "Weebles wobble, but they don't fall down."

The good news is that although our elevators are old, there is an emergency box in it, just in case you get stuck. Someone was thinking ahead in the lift design department. From what I have observed, the squawk box works. I have seen our building attendant shouting into the box on several occasions. Fortunately that day, I missed out on the fun and walked up to the tenth floor. Ingrid, however, was not so fortunate. She was on the lift when it stopped between the 1st and 2nd floors. I do not know if the squawk box worked, but Ingrid told me that yelling really loud, "I'm stuck! Help me!" worked. Her ordeal was short-lived.

Here is some more good news: since the elevators randomly do not work, I quickly developed my vocabulary to assess whether I was going to have to walk up and down the stairs, which is another adventure. You better have a flashlight on you at all times because there isn't any lighting in the stairwell. Someone in the architectural design department was not thinking ahead. Anyway, I quickly learned the word for elevator (lift, pronounced l-eee-ft) and figured out how to ask our building attendant if the lift was working today as well as "Will the lift work tomorrow? Will the lift work this afternoon? When will the lift work?" Her response in Russian: "Only God knows." My Russian teacher would be pleased with my efforts. Now, if I can only figure out how to post a picture of the NCDOL inspector in the elevator and click my heels three times as I enter the lift, I will feel much better.

Making Change

I have developed a new skill over the past three months; I can stare at a person for a long period of time, acting like I do not care, and still be nice about it. Let me explain. Normally when you enter a business, you assume that the owner of the business wants you to buy something. Since they want your money, they try to offer quality goods and decent customer service at a reasonable price. The business does what it can to get you to open up your wallet.

This mentality does not exist in other parts of the world. For example, in the past, when Americans would go to Budapest on business, while in the city, they would buy crock pots, an item that was not available than in Kyiv. After a while, the store stopped selling the crockpots despite the fact that they were selling extremely well. An American who lived in Budapest asked the store why they did not have any more crockpots. The manager said that too many people were buying them up and, therefore, the store had to constantly order more and couldn't keep one on the shelf for display. It was just too much work. I wonder if it ever occurred to them to raise the price of the crockpots.

Anyway, I have discovered that the customer is not always king here. I was at a nice supermarket buying $125 worth of groceries. I chose a line and waited for the rite of passage ritual to begin. First, you must make sure that the red bar is not on the conveyor belt. That means the register is closing. Look for the white bar and use it so that your items are separated from the customer in front of you. While waiting for your turn, you estimate how many bags and what size bags you will need for your groceries. You pay for the bags, so this is a crucial calculation. Also, if you run out of bags, it quickly becomes a bad shopping day. Second, the person at the register will ask you if you need a bag or bags and what size. I am ready since I have used my time wisely. Third, you will be asked if you have a store card. I do not, although I made an attempt once. I wanted to be able to flash my red store card and, of course, get a discount.

I asked how to get a card and was told that I had to go to register one with my passport and receipt. Fair enough. When I arrived at register one, I assumed that I was going to complete a good shopping day. I was wrong. I asked for a store card and gave the woman my passport and receipt. After inspecting my documents, she told me that I had to spend at least 1,000 griven at one time to get a card. I had only spent 960 griven. If only I had bought more M&M's! I was about $5 short, and she was not going to let that slide. How do I solve this problem? My friend had just finished checking out, and he had spent more than 1,000 griven, so I got his receipt and brought it to register one. Who cares whose receipt it is? The woman inspected the receipt and rejected it because my friend already had a card, so his bill had already been credited to a store card. Nice try.

Anyway, there I am in line, and the woman starts scanning my groceries. At this point, you take your bags and start filling them up. They do not bag for you, and I am not sure why since it would employ more people, which appears to be the goal in some of these stores. I have never seen so many employees assigned to each row in the supermarket. They stand there doing nothing until you take a jar of tomato sauce off the shelf, and then they burst into action and restore order to the shelf. I still have not figured out why there are three employees hovering in the fresh bread section. At least they do bag your bread for you. I want to ask them if they have been trained to bag other products besides bread. If so, I have an idea of what they could do.

Bagging your own groceries is always an adventure, and the pressure is on. They can scan your stuff faster than you can pack it unless you buy a package of instant coffee—then the show stops, and you may not make it out alive. This is a devious strategy, though, and should only be used in case of an emergency—the registered employee is mean to you.

I did this once but out of complete ignorance. I bought a pack of vanilla-flavored instant coffee that contained ten individual packets in that package. These packs keep my brain going during Russian school. You can never have enough coffee while studying Russian; it will keep you awake and is a safer alternative to alcohol. The price for the package listed on the shelf was around 10 griven. When the employee saw the package, she froze. She asked me if I had a single-packet of vanilla-flavored instant coffee. I replied, "Oh, no." I had to go get a single-packet so she could ring it up and then multiple by ten. The customers behind me were not thrilled. After this disaster, I now bring a single-packet in addition to the ten-pack to avoid giving the employee at the register a heart attack. Of course, she then asks me if I want to buy the single-packet in addition to the ten-pack. "Oh, yeah! Why not? Let me make your day. I do not want to return it."

Well, I get all my groceries bagged, and now I have to pay. I am getting much better with numbers, but fortunately, I can see the amount on the cashier's computer. This particular day, the total was something like 957.33 griven. I pull out five, 200 griven bills, for a total of 1,000 griven. This is easy, quick, and simple. I hand over the money, she puts the bills under a light to check if they are authentic and then asks me if I have exact change or at least 33 kopeks. Getting change in this country is a big deal. You have to fight for it. Everyone needs small bills, particularly for the marshrutka, but no one seems to have them.

I look at the woman and think, "What is the deal? I thought stores were supposed to have change. People, known as customers, are coming through here all the time, giving you money, and they just might need some change once in a while. You have lots of banks here. I am only asking for $5 change. There are twenty registers flush with cash. Has there been a run on kopeks lately that I missed? Just give me my change so I can get out of here."

She asks me again for change, and then I give her the stare. I smile and with my stare, say, "I do not have the exact amount, I am not looking in my wallet for the exact change even if I have it, and you did not hear change jingling in my pocket as I jogged to get that single packet for you, so too bad." We are at a stalemate, and I am wondering if the security guard is going to be called in to mediate the situation. What are they going to do, take all my groceries back? She finally pushes the button, and I hear the magical ring of the cash register. I have some precious change and am free at last.

Missing Card

It is always an adventure living in Kyiv. The other week I went to use my bank card to withdraw money from the ATM, and the card was not in my wallet, but everything else was there, including my precious Ukrainian currency, known as griven. There is just something about the word grieve referring to money that is odd, but perhaps true. Anyway, I looked around the apartment, checked my jacket, emptied out my pockets, and looked under the boys' bed, but could not locate the card. In the meantime, I checked my bank account in case someone had stolen my card. To my relief, I had not purchased any caviar or plane tickets to the Caribbean online.

I knew where I had last used the card (close to our apartment), and Ingrid suggested that maybe I had left the card in the ATM. Anything is possible since learning Russian causes you to do all sorts of strange things, and I am a professor. Ingrid thought that we should go to Broke Business Bank (I like that name) and see if they had my card. Yeah, right. What are the chances? I had nothing to lose, so we went, and I explained in Russian that I was an idiot. I might have lost my card in the ATM at this bank on Thursday night, but I am not sure and hope I win the lottery. Who can I talk to? Incredibly, the guard understood me and told us to go back outside and go in the next door. We located the bank office, and I sat down at one of the windows in front of a woman and repeated my "I am a potential idiot routine."

To say the least, she was confused. Of course, the situation caused the confusion, certainly not my Russian (LOL). She asked if the card belonged to Broke Business Bank. Nyet. I could never bank here because of the name. I told her it was an American bank card. Now she was really confused. She asked me if I was visiting Kyiv. I told her that I lived here. She seemed amazed and perplexed, but she did not believe me and was trying to figure out what kind of scam I was working. She did, however, check her files for missing cards, and my card was not there. I told her again that I used my card at the ATM located about 20 feet away, and I might have forgotten to take my card on Thursday night. She asked me about what time, and I said, "19:00." I suggested to her that maybe the card is in the machine.

She got up and left and returned a minute later with my card! These Russian lessons are paying off! But then things got interesting. She was not going to give me my card back! After all that fine Russian, you are going to leave me hanging? Are you really going to try to mail that card back to America? What are you going to do with it anyway? She had to check with her boss since I am sure this situation was not covered in the employee manual. After some discussion, she had me show her my passport, give her my phone number, and sign about 100 forms. After the paperwork was completed, she returned my card to me. What are the odds?

A Funny Thing Happened on the Way to Vienna

One day, we began our pursuit of a new residence permit to live in Ukraine for another year. What were we thinking? We arrived at the Kyiv airport around 5 PM, and our plane was delayed for three hours. We arrived at the Eden House (the guest house) in Budapest, Hungary, around 1 AM and received a debriefing on the policies and procedures for the guest house because our hosts had to go to language lessons in the morning. We stumbled into bed and set the alarm so that we could buy some food in the morning, eat breakfast, and head to the embassy by 9 AM.

Though a bit tired, all was going well. We arrived early at the Ukrainian Embassy and were first in a line. At nine o'clock, the guard buzzed us in, and we triumphantly approached the door. We had our documents, photos, and passports. We were prepared. We entered, went to a window, and waited for a civil servant to appear. I noticed, however, that it was not the window for visas. A civil servant appeared, and we told her in Russian that we were here to get new visas to live in Ukraine. She replied in Russian that the embassy was not issuing visas until August. My Russian is not that great, but I understood what she had said, but refused to believe it and assumed that I did not just hear her correctly.

Certainly, my ears and brain were playing tricks on me. We smiled and asked again, somehow expecting a different response. We received that same response just a little bit slower to ensure that we understood. We asked why, and she did not give us an answer. I think the visa man was on vacation or fired. Who knows? Maybe only one person processes visas, and when he or she is out, you are about to have a bad day.

She suggested trying some other city in Hungary closer to Ukraine. I asked where is the closest embassy would issue visas? She suggested Bratislava, and we said Vienna? She said she would check on Vienna for us. She returned and gave us the information for the Ukrainian Embassy in Vienna. She seemed quite optimistic that in either city we could get the visas.

HOW TO GET FIVE UKRAINIANS IN A DRYER

We noted that our letter of invitation from the Ministry of Religious Affairs specifically said Budapest. She read it and looked at us and said, "You are right," but did not think it would be a problem since her embassy was not giving out visas.

When our logistics office in Kyiv called the embassy in Budapest a few weeks ago and inquired about getting visas, no mention was made that July is an evil month to try to get visas. All was well, and so we headed off to Budapest, unaware of the impending, inexplicable closing of the visa office. As we left the embassy, the lady mentioned that we were not the first people that this happened to the Ukrainian Embassy in Budapest. I felt so much better.

We decided to head off immediately for Vienna so that we could be there first thing Tuesday morning. In Vienna, we had friends to stay with, great public transportation, and we can speak the language. We thought these facts should make things easier. We headed to the train station in Budapest, bought train tickets to Vienna, and grabbed a bite to eat at a place the flame-broils their burgers. The train was nice, and we made it to our friends around 5 PM.

The next morning, we trekked about an hour to the Ukrainian Embassy via a tram, to the metro, to tram, and a five-minute walk up the hill. Not too bad. We exchanged the customary Russian greetings with the guard, and he opened the gate. After about 20 minutes, it was our turn at the window. We explained that we lived in Kyiv and wanted to apply to get new visas. So far, so good.

Here is a summary of the conversation (and my thoughts) that ensued:

> NOT LISTENING LADY: Where do you live in Austria?
> US: Uh, we don't. We live in Kyiv.
>
> CATCHING ON LADY: OK. Where are you from?
> US: The United States and Germany. We are schizophrenics.
>
> CONFUSED LADY: Why are you here then if you are not from Austria?
> US: Good question! We were wondering about the same thing. The embassy in Budapest was not giving visas and said to come here since you are open.
>
> PERPLEXED LADY: Why would you go to Budapest if you are American or German? How can they give you a visa? You are supposed to go to your home country to get new visas. Why are they not giving out visas anyway?
> US: I wish I knew, but I don't. I am not an expert on inconsistencies among Ukrainian Embassies on foreign soil. I will have to get back to

you on that, but our American friends go to Budapest and get visas, and they are not Hungarian. That embassy issues visas to foreigners.

RELUCTANT LADY: Give me your paperwork and passports and write a note explaining the situation. Maybe we can do something. You will have to get an AIDS test and pay 178 Euros each. We will call you.
US: Thanks. Can we get the visas by Friday?

Nothing really happened for two days. Our logistics office had to send another letter of invitation addressed to the Austrian embassy, and we waited during the mornings for an answer. We needed an answer soon because we had flights out of Budapest for Sunday. On Wednesday morning, we spoke with the lady, and she informed us that they had to call Budapest to confirm that they were not issuing visas. What? Why would we come to Austria, pay more money, have to get an AIDS test, and bother you? I know you are doing your job, but who would make this stuff up? I think they just wanted to find out what was going on in Budapest.

In the meantime, back on the home front, our neighbors called our landlord, telling him that water was running in our apartment. Our landlord and logistics expert met at 2 AM at our apartment to check things out, but they did not have a key. The landlord shut the water off from the roof that night and then checked our place out Thursday (a friend had a key). Apparently, a flood was expected, but all was well. We are still not 100% sure what happened since I had shut off all the water valves before leaving for Budapest. One of those great mysteries.

On Wednesday afternoon, we heard via our office in Kyiv that we had about an 80% chance of getting the visas. Thursday morning, the lady called us at 9:05 AM and said we could get the visas Friday morning, providing we bring the results of the AIDS test, the receipt for payment, and call her within three hours that we completed those two tasks. Wow! Our children were not looking forward to the blood test, and I had told them earlier not to worry about it since it may never happen. Now I looked like a liar. I asked Ingrid to call the embassy and find out if all of us had to get the aids test. Nope, only the adults. A cheer erupted in the apartment. I leaned over to Evelyn and said, "See, I was right! Always trust your father." She replied, "You got lucky!"

Our friends knew of an excellent medical laboratory nearby that could do the test. I assumed in a socialist country, these would be fairly easy and cheap, maybe even free. Everyone has a right to an AIDS test nowadays. I was partially right about this. We arrived, and I thought about telling the nurse that I just got stabbed on the street by a thug with a needle and needed instantaneous results, but that would not be the truth, though effective. We paid about $36 total, and the nurse said we could have the results in about five hours. Awesome. It took about ten minutes to complete the process, and our technician was great. When she found out that I was a seminary professor and could ramble off the German, she suggested that I apply in Austria at Catholic monasteries. She thought it may take some time to get a response, but it would be worth the effort. I did not want to say anything since she had the needle in my arm. She was really nice, though.

We then headed off to the back. The problem was that we needed a lot of money, and we could only get about $1,000 per day from the ATM. We tried several possibilities with the bank (VISA card) but ultimately took money from the ATM and borrowed the rest from our friends. Interestingly, in order to pay, you need your passport for identification, which of course were at the embassy. Another classic bureaucratic Catch-22, but in this case, I was going insane regardless of the circumstances. Our friend Lance alerted us to the vicious cycle ahead of time, and we came prepared. Ingrid bailed us out since she has two passports and only gave one to the embassy. We finished everything in record time and called the lady by 12 PM. I went Friday morning to pick everything up at the embassy without any problems. We were now proud owners of visas and on our way back to Budapest.

On Saturday, we saw Budapest, caught a film in English, and I found Subway. First real roast beef sandwich in fifteen months. It was good. On Sunday morning, we woke up at 5:30 AM and headed to the airport, arriving around 6:30 AM for an 8:45 AM flight. The problem is that we did not see our flight on the departure board. Here we go again, another delay. In this case, however, the damage was self-inflicted by none other than *moi*. I checked the itinerary again after chatting with an online agent and discovered that our flight was scheduled for 8:45 PM. Yikes!

This was not a huge problem except that it was about 60 degrees and raining. Ingrid said, "Well, you are just like your father. You do not make mistakes real often, but when you do, you make big ones!" She was referring to my father's legendary gaffe in France in 1995. It is part of the family folklore now, and just about everyone knows the story, and if they do not, they will now. Welcome to the family. Even my children know the story as if they were there, which is impossible since we got married in 1995, thus the reason my family was in France (sightseeing before the wedding). Anyway, my father accidentally filled the rental van up with the wrong gas (diesel instead of regular or vice versa), and the rental van did not make it very far. In his defense, the gas pump fit in the gas tank, and with a 50% chance, he just guessed wrong. There was no indication in the van or in the paperwork. It can happen to anyone. Still, it makes for a good rental car story.

Anyway, my kids laughed and thought it was funny, and I now, following in my father's footsteps, will be reminded of my legendary gaffe in Budapest. When you get something stuck in your head, it just stays there. Unlike my father, however, I did not destroy someone's property. I digress. We headed into the city and went to the indoor aquarium, a coffee house, and IKEA. We departed on time and arrived in Kyiv, where I nearly hit a parked car driving out of the parking lot. Fortunately, all was fine and arrived home safely around 1 AM. When we opened the refrigerator to get something to drink, the odor set our olfactory nerves on fire. Someone had accidentally unplugged it on Thursday while ensuring that there was not a flood. Ukrainians are real particular about shutting off the water valves and unplugging everything while on vacation. Just a little overzealous in this case. It was an appropriate ending to an adventure-filled week, but we had our visas!

CHAPTER 6
EPILOGUE

I hope you enjoyed the stories. We have lived in Ukraine for twelve years and lived in both the capital Kyiv and the beautiful city in the West, L'viv. After the first year, life was easier as we adapted to the culture and figured out how life works in Ukraine. Learning the language helped and, of course, making friends. If you want to live overseas, it does take humility and the ability to laugh at yourself. I highly recommend living overseas and exploring new cultures. If you do, you will enlarge your view of the world and see your own culture with a new perspective.

If you enjoyed the book, please leave an honest review on Amazon for me. Greatly appreciate it!

ABOUT THE AUTHOR

Dr. Russell Woodridge and his family moved to Ukraine in 2009. He and his wife, Ingrid, have four children and have been married twenty-five years. He is Academic Dean of Ukrainian Baptist Theological Seminary and is coauthor of The Prosperity Gospel, which has been translated into Spanish and Russian. The stories are based on his experience in Ukraine.

www.ingramcontent.com/pod-product-compliance
Lightning Source LLC
Chambersburg PA
CBHW061345040426
42444CB00011B/3090